This book belongs to

· ·

flower

boat

dog

duck

moon

egg

First published 2011 by Brown Watson
The Old Mill, 76 Fleckney Road,
Kibworth Beauchamp, Leic LE8 0HG

ISBN: 978-0-7097-1927-4

My First
Words

kite

lion

bird

tractor

Brown Watson

ENGLAND

flower

boat

fish

duck

egg

cat

ball

car

cup

bee

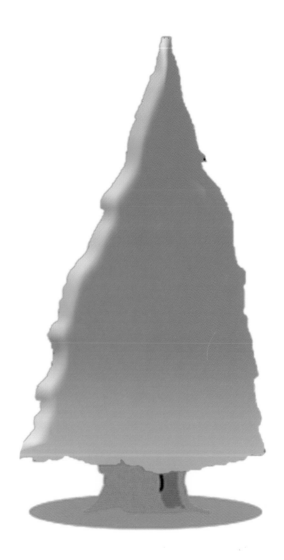

tree

spoon

COW

boy

bird

moon

toys

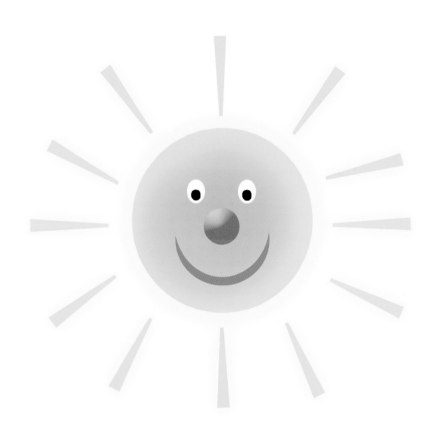

sun

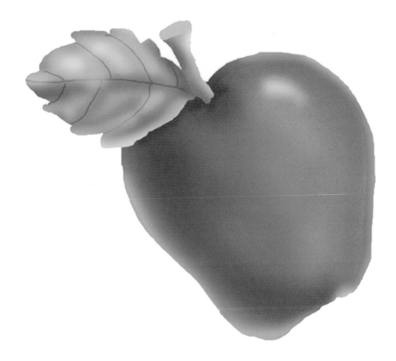

apple

girl

dog

bed

train

teddy